WE WANT YOU TO KNOW WHAT PEOPLE ARE SAYING ABOUT SKINNY ON BOOKS!!!

The Mercury News

The Newspaper of Silicon Valley
MercuryNews.com

Here is one example, an excerpt from a September, 2009 article, in the respected Silicon Valley newspaper, The Mercury News.

"It's my angry belief that most self-help and education book writers get paid by the word. Actually, it's worse than that. Most get paid by the character. This means lots of pointlessly long words, ridiculously complex sentences and page after page after page – you get the idea – of drivel. Three and four hundred page books that could have been done better in 50 pages.

No wonder college students sleep until noon. It isn't the sex, drugs, and rock and roll. No way! they have to read this garbage every day! Personally, I'd rather read the phone book.

Not so with 'The Skinny On' series. These books kick rears and take names. Using entertaining writing, stick figure drawings and a comic book style layout, they use simple stories to quickly convey valuable information.

Each book is like a university class without the fuddy-duddy professor. YIPPEE! Each slender, practical, engaging book can be read in an hour or so. And each gives the kind of advice you might get from a kindly, extremely knowledgeable grandfather.

Highly recommended. Author Jim Randel has created one of the best, most interesting series I've seen in a very long time."

the skinny on™

time management

how to maximize your 24-hour gift

Jim Randel

ISBN: 978-0-9841393-9-2
Library of Congress: 2009910878

Illustration: Malinda Nass

For information address RAND Publishing, 265 Post Road West, Westport, CT, 06880 or call (203) 226-8727.

The Skinny On™ books are available for special promotions and premiums. For details contact: Donna Hardy, call (203) 222-6295 or visit our website: www.theskinnyon.com

Printed in the United States of America

10 9 8 7 6 5 4 3 2 1
9 2 5 – 4 9 1 9

the skinny on™

Welcome to a new series of publications entitled **The Skinny On**™, a progression of drawings, dialogue and text intended to convey information in a concise and entertaining fashion.

In our time-starved and information-overloaded culture, most of us have far too little time to read and absorb important writings and research on topics of interest to us. So, our understanding tends to float on the surface – without the insights of leaders and teachers who have spent years studying these subjects.

Our series is intended to address this situation. Our team of readers and researchers has done a ton of homework preparing our books for you. We read everything we could find on the topic at hand and spoke with the experts. Then we mixed in our own experiences and distilled what we have learned into this "skinny" book for your benefit.

Our goal is to do the reading for you, identify what is important, distill the key points, and present them in a book that is both instructive and entertaining.

Although minimalist in design, we do take our message very seriously. Please do not confuse format with content. The time you invest reading this book will be paid back to you many, many times over.

INTRODUCTION

We at **The Skinny On** books believe that less is more. We believe that too many writers, thinkers and researchers tend to use 10 words when 5 will do. Perhaps that is historical. Since books have always been pretty hefty items, writers see no reason to change what has worked in the past.

We don't believe that what worked in the past should be the way of the future. Heck, screaming from one neighbor to another may have been an adequate form of communication 200 years ago, but today cell phones are generally preferable.

Our objective is to completely research a particular subject – in this case **time management** – and then to distill for you, the reader, just what you need to know. Not all the fluff … not all the filler. Just what you need to know.

We have read about 100 books and articles on **time management** and here is what we learned: the process was a waste of time! All the writings say pretty much the same thing. The fact is that there are about 50 principles of **time management** that you need to know … and once you learn those, you have learned what you need to know about this subject. All 50 of these principles are addressed in this book.

We are asking for JUST one hour of your time to read our book. We assure you that reading our book will be one of the best expenditures of your time that you have ever made.

"Time is the quality of nature that keeps events from happening all at once. Lately it doesn't seem to be working so well."

Anonymous

Hi, I am Jim Randel. I am the founder of **The Skinny On** book series. I will be your guide for the next hour.

Welcome to my home. I've converted my garage into a classroom, and I'd like to use it today to teach you about time management.

Notice the bikes. They are there for a reason. One, I like to bike. Two, I want you to understand that although time management is a critical factor in one's success, that does not mean good time managers spend their life darting from one activity to the other. There are instances when I ride my bike to places just because I enjoy a slow bike ride.

Today we are going to discuss how to make the best use of your time so to optimize the probability that you will achieve your goals. I won't suggest you give up biking or walking or gazing at the stars. I just want you to understand the importance of using time effectively … as and when you desire to.

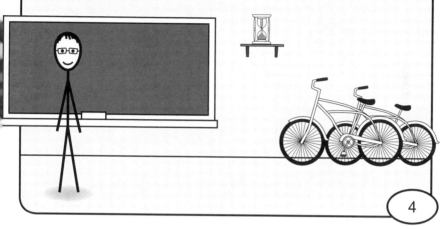

Time is a quickly moving asset. You only have so much of it. What you do with the time you have will be critical to your future.

In many ways, time is your most valuable commodity – waste it at your risk.

Everyone gets 168 hours a week or about 720 hours per month.

Every hour counts.

That's why I have this hour glass. I want you to be able to finish my course in just 60 minutes. I don't want to waste one minute of your time.

This is you. We know that you really look a lot better than this.

By the end of our time together you will have a smile on your face because you will have a much better understanding of time management.

WHAT IS TIME MANAGEMENT?

TIME MANAGEMENT IS THE APPLICATION OF STRATEGIES AND TECHNIQUES TO HELP YOU USE YOUR TIME AS EFFECTIVELY AS POSSIBLE.

8

1. IN THE FIRST HALF OF OUR CLASS, WE WILL REVIEW **HOW YOU ARE PRESENTLY SPENDING YOUR TIME**.

Are you aware of where the hours are going? Are you spending time in a way to move you closer to your goals? Are you making good choices?

2. IN THE SECOND HALF OF OUR CLASS, WE WILL ANALYZE WHETHER YOU ARE **USING THE HOURS YOU HAVE TO MAXIMUM EFFECTIVENESS**.

Once you are aware of how you presently consume your time, you need to determine whether you are using time as effectively as possible. The objective is not just spending time in the right places, but also using the hours you have as powerfully as possible.

9

PART I

A REVIEW OF HOW YOU ARE SPENDING YOUR TIME

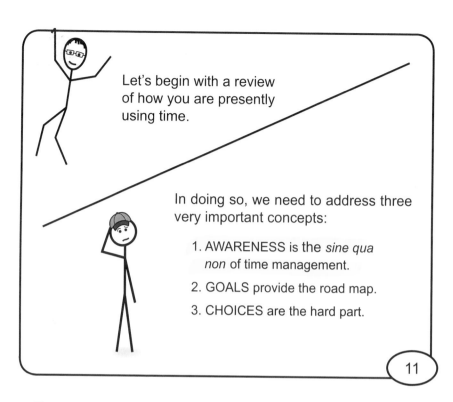

Let's begin with a review of how you are presently using time.

In doing so, we need to address three very important concepts:

1. AWARENESS is the *sine qua non* of time management.

2. GOALS provide the road map.

3. CHOICES are the hard part.

AWARENESS

You cannot be an effective time manager unless you are attuned to the passage of time. I wear a runner's watch 24 hours a day because I like to see the seconds flying by – that helps remind me of how quickly time passes!

As a first exercise, I would like you to write down your best guess as to how you spent the last 72 hours. Make general categories and assign hours to each category.

This does not have to be super precise. It's just meant to start you thinking.

Here is a chart you can use. Or create your own.

Sleeping:	_____ hours
Eating:	_____ hours
Study/Reading:	_____ hours
Watching TV:	_____ hours
Online:	_____ hours
Phone/Texting:	_____ hours
Exercise:	_____ hours
Class or work time:	_____ hours
Recreation:	_____ hours
Miscellaneous:	_____ hours
TOTAL:	**72 hours**

In the past I have kept a time journal. At the end of every day for one week, I would take a moment before going to bed to write down precisely how I spent the preceding 24 hours. I did this because I wanted to know exactly how I was spending my time in 30-minute increments.

#1 Awareness is the Sine Qua Non

HERE IS WHAT ONE DAY IN MY TIME JOURNAL LOOKS LIKE:

Time Management Evaluation

TIME	MONDAY	TUESDAY	WEDNESDAY
Midnight			
12:30			
1:00am			
1:30	Sleep		
2:00am			
2:30			
3:00am			
3:30			
4:00am			
4:30			
5:00am			
5:30	Write		
6:00am			
6:30			
7:00am			
7:30			
8:00am	Breakfast–		
8:30	Shower–		
9:00am	Dress		
9:30			
10:00am			
10:30			
11:00am	Research		
11:30			
NOON			
12:30			
1:00pm	Lunch		
1:30			
2:00pm			
2:30			
3:00pm	Phone – Email		
3:30			
4:00pm			
4:30	Exercise		
5:00pm			
5:30			
6:00pm	Dinner		
6:30			
7:00pm			
7:30	Baseball game		
8:00pm	on T.V.		
8:30			
9:00pm			
9:30			
10:00pm	Read		
10:30			
11:00pm	Sleep		
11:30			

Then at the end of the week, I totaled how much time I spent in various general categories.

Sleeping:	49 hours
Eating:	15 hours
Study/Reading (research):	10 hours
Watching TV (sports):	15 hours
Online (e-mails):	7 hours
Phone/texting:	5 hours
Exercise:	10 hours
Class or Work Time (writing):	40 hours
Recreation (meditation, biking):	7 hours
Miscellaneous:	10 hours
TOTAL:	168 hours

16

And you know what? I surprised myself by how much time I was spending watching sports. As it happens, I was spending about 15 hours of every week watching sports. I decided this was too much if I was going to keep to my schedule of writing 6 books a year.

I realized that if I cut back my TV time to 7.5 hours per week, I would have about 30 additional hours every month in which to write, or 360 hours per year. In that time I could write one or two more books.

17

Does it seem odd to you that I did not know how much time I was spending watching sports? In one way, I did know of course. It's just that by forcing myself to total up the hours – as against the 168 hours I had in the week – I confronted the fact that I was spending almost 13% of my waking hours watching sports.

Certain activities are seductive of course. We do them with all good intentions to limit ourselves to a certain amount of time. And then, whoosh … time flies. We lose track of time and we spend more than planned.

I am sure that you have heard of Albert Einstein. He is famous for many things including the theory of relativity, E = MC squared, which basically means … well, actually I have no idea what it means. But, no matter, I have my own theory of relativity.

My theory of relativity says that how we experience time depends upon what we are doing. I have indicated that I lose track of time when I am watching sports on TV. Minutes pass quickly. But, when I come home at the end of a day, starving, and throw something into the microwave, a five-minute wait seems like forever.

My point here is that you need to be aware of how you experience time. What are you doing when time flies? When it drags?

An awareness of how you experience time can tell you a lot about yourself.

How a person experiences time is a window into his or her true passions. The objective is to balance your consumption of time in a way that meshes goals and passions. I love sports but too much gets in the way of my need and desire to write. On the other hand, if I spend too much time writing, it becomes drudgery for me which impacts the quality of what I do.

Self-awareness is critical for three reasons:

1. By increasing awareness as to how you spend time, you may discover areas where adjustments are appropriate. For example, my decision to reduce the time I was watching sports.

2. By gaining a better understanding of how you spend time, you may find opportunities to pick up productive time. Trying to be helpful, just the other day I mentioned to my wife that her average daily shower was 15 minutes, and that if she could get it down to ten minutes, she could pick up an additional 2.5 hours of productive time every month. She told me that if I ever brought that up again, she would hit me.

3. Just by focusing on time, by keeping a journal, you start to think of time as a fleeting asset. Making a journal sensitizes you as to how you are spending your depreciating asset – the hours of your life.

OK, now that you understand the importance of awareness do you want to take a guess at the meaning of the Latin expression *sine qua non*?

Sine Qua Non

The translation of sine qua non is **without which, nothing.**

It means that if you do not have an awareness of how you are spending time, you have no ability to manage your time effectively. There is no point fooling yourself.

That is why self-awareness is the first step!

GOALS

OK, time is flying. We now need to discuss the second concept --- by defining goals, we begin to highlight the route we need to take.

#2 Goals provide the road map

"Goals are the fuel in the furnace of achievement."

Anonymous

You can't decide where you should allocate your time unless and until you determine exactly where it is you want to go. That is why I call goal setting the road map.

Goal setting is about deciding today where you want to be, and what you want to be doing, say in 6 months… or one year… or five years.

There is no accepted standard as to what is a short-term goal and what is a longer-term goal. Just so we have something to work with, let's call any goal that can be achieved within one year a short-term goal, and all other goals long-term.

For purposes of our discussion, let's also distinguish a goal from a task. When I use the word "task," I am speaking to a chore or job or errand that must be accomplished in the very near term.

On your To Do List you put tasks, on your Mission Statement you put goals.

One of my objectives with this book is to get you thinking... about your goals, your dreams, your best-case scenario.

You

"What are your goals? What do you hope to accomplish in the short term? What do you want your life to look like in the long term?

"How do you plan on getting from where you are to where you want to be? What are the steps from here to there?"

Who knew he'd be asking such difficult questions in a course on time management? I need some time to reflect.

I don't mean to be intrusive but if you don't know where you want your life to be in the near and far term, then you don't know what steps you must take, and what kind of time you need to allocate to each step.

Once you have identified your goals, you can better identify the steps you need to take, and the time commitments you need to make.

#2 Goals provide the road map

THE FOLLOWING IS AN EXAMPLE OF A GOALS-STEPS-TIME ANALYSIS I DID RECENTLY WITH MY COLLEGE-AGED DAUGHTER.

WHAT IS IMPORTANT IS THAT YOU SEE THE PROCESS OF CONNECTING GOALS AND TIME.

My daughter's goal was to obtain a 3.5 GPA in the fall semester of her junior year. Her goal met what experts identify as the four most important criteria of a goal:

(i) it was specific (3.5 GPA),

(ii) it had a time frame (fall semester),

(iii) it was realistic (she knew she was capable), and

(iv) it was important to the goal-setter (this was my daughter's idea).

My daughter will be taking 12 credits in the fall. That means 12 hours of class time per week. She decided that she would need to spend 2.5 hours of time outside class for every hour in class if she was going to achieve a 3.5 GPA. The 2.5 hours included class assignments, preparation, reading, and study time for tests and quizzes. So that means another 30 hours per week (12 x 2.5).

So, total school time = 42 hours (class and outside class).

Then my daughter listed all her other activities during the week and the hours she needed for each.

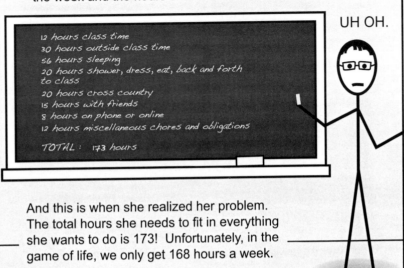

12 hours class time
30 hours outside class time
56 hours sleeping
20 hours shower, dress, eat, back and forth to class
20 hours cross country
15 hours with friends
8 hours on phone or online
12 hours miscellaneous chores and obligations

TOTAL : 173 hours

UH OH.

And this is when she realized her problem. The total hours she needs to fit in everything she wants to do is 173! Unfortunately, in the game of life, we only get 168 hours a week.

33

This analysis showed my daughter that if she really wanted to achieve a 3.5 GPA, she was going to have to make some changes in how she spends her time. Perhaps she will have to sleep less. Or spend less time eating and dressing for school. Or cut back on the hours she spends with friends.

#2 Goals provide the road map

34

I am using this example to make a point. Whatever your goal there will be action steps you need to take to achieve it. Those steps will take time. Do you have the time? Are you prepared to take time from other activities in order to find the time you need?

#2 Goals provide the road map

But what if I don't know all the steps I need to take to achieve my goals? What if I don't know the time I need for the steps I do know?

"Excellent question ... I am happy to see that you are paying such careful attention and that you are thinking about what I am saying."

There may be several steps between where you are and where you want to be that are either unknown or not clear to you. That's fine. Just by beginning to contemplate the passage, three important things start to happen.

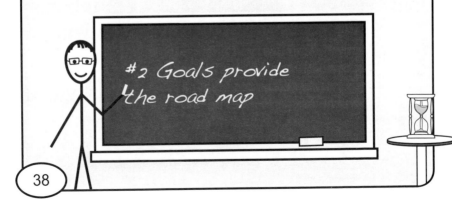

#2 Goals provide the road map

First, just by thinking about steps and time, you engage your analytical and creative juices. You move the ball forward in understanding what you have to do to get where you want to be.

Second, whether you realize it or not, you are starting to plan. You are starting to actually visualize the achievement of your goals. Visualization increases desire which increases intensity.

Third, you are testing your resolve. By identifying specific steps and time requirements, you double check your intensity for certain goals. There may be situations, in fact, when you make a conscious decision to put off the pursuit of one of your goals because you conclude you don't have the desire to do what is required to go from here to there.

All I am trying to do at this point in our session is to help you conceptualize a goals-steps-time analysis.

This is not an exact science. I am just suggesting you begin the process of integrating goal-setting and time management.

LET'S RECAP:

1. BY BECOMING MORE **AWARE** OF HOW YOU ARE USING TIME, YOU IDENTIFY SPACES WHERE YOU MAY WANT TO MAKE CHANGES.

2. BY DEFINING YOUR **GOALS**, YOU ESTABLISH A ROAD MAP FOR THE PASSAGE FROM HERE TO THERE.

41

CHOICES

All of this leads to the third major concept with respect to your use ... or abuse ... of time. Dreams don't come easily, choices need to be made.

#3 Choices are the hard part

42

Once you are aware of how you use time and have a road map of your goals, the nuts and bolts of the analysis are complete. Now, however, comes the tough part.

Now you need to do a gut check. You need to find a balance between living for the moment – doing exactly what you want to do right now. And, living for the future – putting yourself in a position to lead the life you want at some point down the road.

I need to get closer to you right now. I need to tell you something really important about life: **LIFE IS NOT FAIR**.

I am not going to stand here and tell you that if you work very hard you can be anything you want. Life just does not work that way. There are factors and events beyond your control that will impact how your life plays out.

But what I can tell you is this: by making the right choices, by putting yourself in a position to succeed, you maximize the chances you will achieve whatever it is that you want.

Time management is in large part about choices. Now that you have a heightened sense of time and have set some goals, you need to confront competing pressures. Calls from friends. The desire to sleep late. Commitments and obligations. The seduction of the internet. Anything that pulls you from what you need to do to achieve your goals.

No one can make those choices but you. Sometimes, those choices are very difficult.

I hope I used mouth wash this morning.

"Successful people do not enjoy doing the things that others do not. Successful people simply do them nevertheless."

The Study of Success, E.N. Gray

At this point in the book I want to introduce you to a very entertaining lecture about time management given by Randy Pausch, formerly Professor of Computer Sciences at Carnegie Mellon.

Professor's Pausch's story is poignant.

At age 40, Professor Pausch, father of 3 young children, learned that he had pancreatic cancer and was dying. He actually lived for 18 months after his diagnosis and during that period he wrote a best-selling book (*The Last Lecture*). He also gave a guest lecture on **time management** at the University of Virginia.

In both his book and his lecture Professor Pausch speaks to choices. He makes the point that life is a constant balancing of competing pressures – living for today, sacrificing for tomorrow.

I think you might enjoy watching Professor Pausch's lecture on time management.

If you'd like to do that, go to youtube and search: "Pausch, University of Virginia."

OK, enough talking … my cell phone is vibrating which means that it is time for me to take a 15 minute break to meditate. I find that if I meditate for just 15 minutes a day, I increase my energy ... and my serenity.

#3 Choices are the hard part

I know that it can be hard to find the 15 minutes to meditate every day. One reason to work hard when you are young is so that later in life you can structure your days exactly as you want them to be.

While I am meditating you might want to take a few minutes to try a fun online self-assessment test which claims to measure what kind of time manager you are. Here's the link:

www.literacynet.org/icans/chapter03/timemgmt.html

When I meditate I play a CD of ocean sounds. I have the CD timed to exactly fifteen minutes so that when it is over, I know that it's time to stop meditating. If I did not do that, I might get lost in thought for hours.

By the way, I don't usually wear blindfolds when I meditate. I just thought it would be a cute visual metaphor for what it's like going through life without an awareness of how you spend your time.

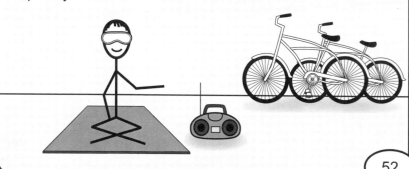

Wow … do I feel refreshed!

You know while I was meditating a thought popped into my head. That happens often … which is one reason to meditate. By quieting the noise, you clear space in your mind for new ideas and thoughts.

The thought is this: **I don't want you to be frantic about not knowing exactly what you want to do with your life.**

For most people goal setting is about identifying general directions. Life often takes twists and turns that none can predict. Still, by constantly reflecting on your goals, and readjusting at times, you increase the probability that your life will proceed on your agenda – and not someone else's or, simply by fate.

"Hey there, Jimmy boy, what you up to today? I hope you're not wasting time. Don't let life happen **to you**, Jimmy boy. Make life happen **for you!**"

Little Jim's Mailman

8-year-old Jim

55

"The secret of success is learning how to use pain and pleasure instead of having pain and pleasure use you. If you do that, you're in control of your life. If you don't, life controls you."

Tony Robbins

Tony Robbins is saying the same thing as Professor Pausch and my mailman. By making conscious choices – between satisfaction and sacrifice – you script your life. By not making choices, you allow other forces to dictate how your life plays out.

56

PART II

USING THE HOURS YOU HAVE
TO MAXIMUM EFFECTIVENESS

We've now come to the midpoint of our class. It's now time to turn to a review of how effective you are with the time you have.

From here on, we are going to talk about strategies and techniques for using what time you do have as powerfully as possible.

I am going to switch to my laptop now and use a screen. I get tired of writing on the blackboard. Blackboards are so yesterday.

Here is the syllabus for Part II of
our session today.

EFFECTIVE AND POWERFUL USE OF TIME

A) You can "create" time.
   (1) Energy
   (2) Watch for gaps.
   (3) Fight off waste.

B) Procrastination is the enemy.

C) Strategies and techniques
   (1) Declutter your mind and life.
   (2) Planning
      a) The magic of To Do lists
      b) The power of prioritizing
   (3) The Power of Focus
   (4) Techniques

In the second half of our class, we are going to learn
the strategies and techniques really successful people
employ to get the most out of every hour.

The first topic I want to discuss is how we can create
more time in our lives.

As you can see, I've typed on the screen, "time is finite." But, wait, didn't I just say that there are ways to create time? How can that be if time is finite? Am I losing my marbles?

Well, perhaps, but here is my point: whereas time is finite, there are ways to turn unproductive time into productive time. That's the same as finding more hours in the day ... of "creating" time for yourself.

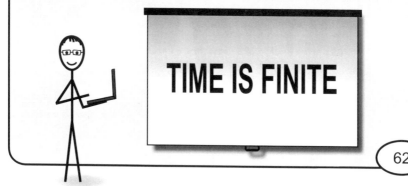

Let me give you an example.

That's what I look like early in the morning when the alarm goes off. Half asleep – half awake. No one enjoys lazing in bed more than I do.

But you know what? By training myself to jump out of bed **as soon as** the alarm goes off instead of laying in bed like I used to, I gain ten minutes a day times 365, or about 60 extra hours of time over the course of a year. That's almost 3 extra days a year of productive time!

OK, OK … I hear you. You don't care about gaining 3 extra days a year. You would rather have 10 additional minutes in bed every morning.

I understand! Notwithstanding what my kids think, I am not "Mr. Always-Be-Productive." Leisure and rest and recreation are critical to a happy life. All I care about is that you are aware of how you spend time, and about the choices you are making.

64

OK, let's go to the next slide. HEY! How did that get in here? My wife must be playing a joke on me. Here, let me get rid of that…

65

Please forgive my wife's little joke. Stick people are not very modest. I don't even know if I'm naked right now. Stick people have debated that subject for years.

MATCHING TIME AND ENERGY

Effective time management is not just about finding additional hours in the day. Impactful time management is also about matching up your available time with your available energy.

To make my point I would like to borrow a phrase from a famous 20th century American writer named Gertrude Stein.

Ms. Stein penned the well-known phrase "a rose is a rose is a rose." Her point was that whatever name you choose to give something, you don't change the essence of what it is. Another way of saying the same thing is that "if it walks like a duck, swims like a duck, and quacks like a duck, it must be a duck."

A ROSE IS A ROSE IS A ROSE

I waddle,
I swim,
I quack.
I must be a duck.

What do Gertrude Stein and ducks have to do with time management? Well they are just set-up's for another concept we need to discuss: **in your pursuit of effective time management, not all hours are alike**.

In order to make each of your hours as effective as possible, you should attempt to perform your hardest tasks in those hours when you are the most alert … when you have the most energy. I happen to be an early bird. I am really flying (excuse the metaphor) at 4 AM and I write well at that hour. But, check back with me at about 10 PM and I can barely talk, let alone write.

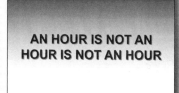

AN HOUR IS NOT AN HOUR IS NOT AN HOUR

My wife on the other hand is a night owl. She hates the early morning. She gets her best work done late at night.

To be very effective, you need to mesh your time slots and energies.

This is me at 10 PM.

You can also take steps to optimize your energy level.

No magic there … exercise daily, eat healthy, get lots of fluids, moderate your intake of stimulants (caffeine) and recreants (alcohol).

With a healthy lifestyle you not only elongate your life, you boost your daily productivity as you turn unproductive hours into productive hours by creating more hours when you have a high energy level.

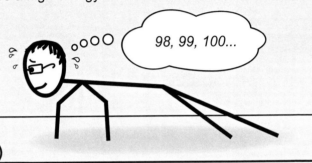

98, 99, 100...

Not bad for an old guy, huh? 100 push-up's at age 60. My goal is actually to do 60 push-up's at age 100! First goal: live to 100.

When do you have your most energy? Use the time when you have the most energy to tackle your ugliest, most difficult chores. In this way you are most likely to finish them in the shortest possible time.   That is effective time management.

GOAL:
AGE: 100
PUSH-UP'S   60

Some experts even suggest that the key to productivity is to focus not on time but on energy. For an excellent book on the time and energy analysis, you might want to pick up:

The Power of Full Engagement: Managing Energy, Not Time, is the Key to High Performance and Personal Renewal

Jim Loehr and Tony Schwartz (Free Press, 2003)

OK. Now let's discuss another area where we can create time: Gap. No, not the store. By "gap" I mean downtime periods. Times when you are waiting for something to happen, and you are cooling your heels in the meantime.

Right after our session today I have to go to the dentist. You may not know this but stick people have a very low pain threshold, and so I really hate the dentist.

76

77

Utilizing downtime while in the dentist's chair is only one example of what I am talking about. We all have gaps in our day. By always having something to do during these gaps, we "create" time by turning unproductive minutes into productive ones.

Please take a few moments to think about gaps in your typical week. Times when are you shuffling your feet, instead of doing something productive. Think of ways to use this time more effectively.

GAPS	HOW TO USE THE GAP MORE EFFECTIVELY
1. _____	1. _____
2. _____	2. _____
3. _____	3. _____

Effective time management is about a minimum of waste. Did you ever notice how great athletes are very fluid. There is little wasted motion or energy.

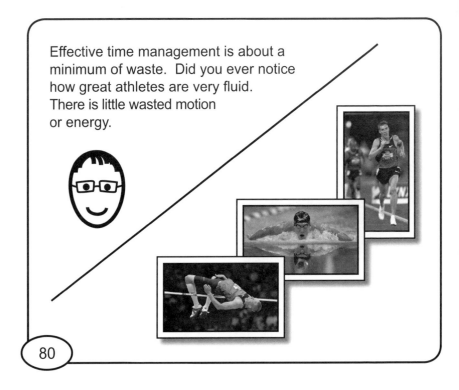

Similarly, great time managers become excellent at minimizing waste. They learn to build efficiency into their lives. Here are three examples of how they do that:

1. Make decisions quickly – tremendous waste comes out of indecision. As soon as you have the facts you need to make a decision, do so.

2. Speed reading – I will be speaking more about this later but here is the key – do not try to read every word of whatever it is you are reading **(except skinny books of course)**. Too many writers use 10 words to communicate when 5 would do. Learn to read just the five.

3. Improve memorization skills. People with good memories operate at a higher level of efficiency than others.

Let's spend a minute or two on memorization skills.

IMPROVING YOUR MEMORY

1. Stretch your mind. I do a crossword puzzle a day. I find that doing so forces me to push myself mentally, to see words and phrases in different ways. To work at my skills of recollection. I am convinced this practice helps my memory. There are tons of puzzles and games you can do. Some people believe video games improve memory.

"Scientists are increasingly examining the potential benefits of video games. Their studies are revealing that a wide variety of games can boost mental function, improving everything from vision to memory."

Boston Globe, **Emily Anthes, October 2009**

2. Spread out your intake of food and drink. When you overload yourself with food and/or drink, your sugar level spikes ... and then shortly thereafter drops dramatically. This causes an energy loss which reduces your mental recall. By taking in less food/drink in any one sitting, you decrease the likelihood of this happening.

3. Exercise. The usual biggie. Exercise increases blood flow to the brain. Studies have shown that exercise reduces the prospect of Alzheimer's. Exercise also has a calming effect which reduces stress and settles the mind.

4. Antioxidants. Foods containing antioxidants, such as berries, broccoli and spinach, appear to improve mental function. Ditto for Omega-3 fatty acids (think fish). We can't say for sure that these food groups will help your memory, but they will make you healthier, so nothing lost!

5. Learn memory skills. I am not great with names so I develop little games for helping me recall a person's name. For example, when I meet a person for the first time, I immediately try to picture him or her with a Post-It note on his/her forehead. On this note is his/her name. For some reason, seeing the name in writing helps me.

"Nice to meet you, YOU."

6. Perform associations or rhymes. The combination on my bike lock is 42-32-10. I had trouble remembering it until I made up a goofy statement for myself:

*"Hey, Jim, you don't look **42**.*
*You don't even look **32**. You're a **10**!"*

OK, silly, I admit
but somehow it
helps me remember!

7. Get enough sleep. There is an expression that "fatigue makes cowards of us all." The point is that we are never at our best when running on empty. That goes for mental productivity as well.

8. Concentrate. I am convinced that one reason people forget things is that they do not concentrate when they first hear a fact, meet a person ... whatever. When you are about to read something that is important to remember, take note and focus. Just that act will improve your powers of recall.

9. Convert important facts into a format that assists your recall. I am always working at improving my vocabulary which is, in part, about memory – i.e., the ability to pull up words to use as and when you want them. One way I do that is by writing down words and definitions that are new to me. I then write down the word in a sentence. The act of writing helps me.

10. Don't stress about your memory skills. Sometimes memory problems come because we stress that we don't have a good memory. It is like a self-fulfilling prophecy: we think we don't have a good memory, so we stress and, **as a result**, we don't have a good memory. You have a better memory than you think. It's just that you can probably make it a little better.

OK, enough about memory skills. Now I must have been making some larger point… I don't remember …

Just goofing! Of course I remember my point: that by utilizing gaps in your day and by cutting down on wasted motion – like indecision, overly slow reading and poor memory – you can make yourself incredibly more efficient.

NOW ON TO A REALLY REALLY BIG TOPIC

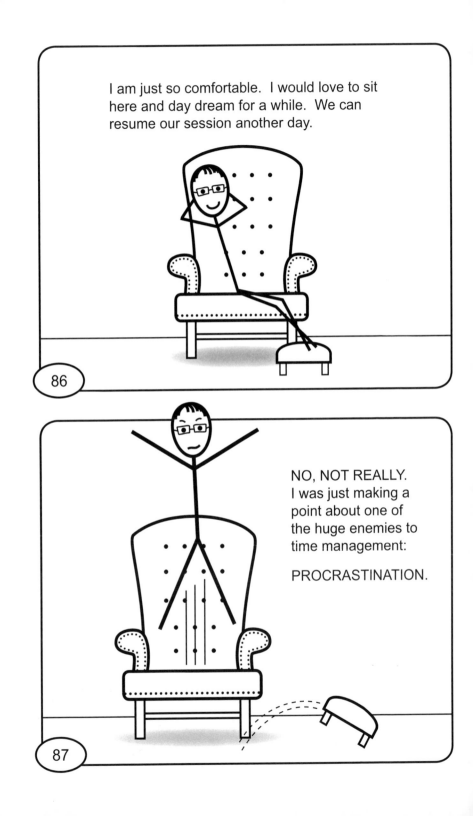

Lots of people have good intentions. They tell you what they are going to do "someday." But "someday" never turns into "today." These people procrastinate their lives away.

"When all is said and done, more is said than done."

Anonymous

Procrastination is the result of a very powerful law of physics known as INERTIA.

Inertia states that a body at rest will remain at rest until acted on by some outside force. In other words, things – including people – tend to stay put. In order to achieve forward motion, people need to push themselves. Inertia tends to keep us all in place.

INERTIA

I used to be a procrastinator. I always had good reasons why not to start on a project or task. Sometimes the magnitude of the project intimidated me. Sometimes I did not know how to start. And sometimes I was just being lazy. In fact, I used to subscribe to Mark Twain's advice:

"Never put off for tomorrow what you can put off until the day after tomorrow."

But then one day it hit me. I was only hurting myself. No one really cared how my life played out … except me. I realized that if I wanted to make something with my life, I needed to stop making excuses.

PROCRASTINATION IS A DREAM KILLER

Little by little, I forced myself to fight back against inertia. I reached a point in my life when an impulse to be lazy was overwhelmed by a fear of looking back with regret on missed opportunities.

INERTIA

STRATEGIES FOR DEFEATING PROCRASTINATION:

1. Keep a piece of paper or index card in your pocket with your goals written in bold ink. People who are adept at warding off procrastination are able to connect the result of their action (or inaction) with the achievement of (or lack thereof) their goals. By keeping reminders of your goals handy, you are less likely to delay steps that can bring you closer to your personal dreamscape.

2. Break big projects up into manageable pieces. Most of us are overwhelmed when contemplating a huge project. We look at the height of the mountain in front of us and we think *"what's the use?"* By dividing that project up into smaller pieces, or by just taking a step forward (even if a small step), the height of the mountain becomes a bit smaller and less intimidating.

3. Train your mind (awareness) to recognize the first signs of laziness or procrastination. We can all feel ourselves getting tired or lazy. We know we should do something but just don't feel like it. When you first begin to experience that feeling, that is the precise time to jump right up and get going. This is an anti-procrastination reflex that can be developed.

4. Always carry a means of taking notes. Your cell phone (or good old-fashioned pad and paper) can be used to memorialize thoughts or ideas. At times you may not have an opportunity to start into a project but you can at least make an outline, or a to do list, or just scribble down some ideas. Putting those thoughts in writing will help propel you into action the next chance you have to get started.

By the way, there is some good news about inertia: it is actually **two** forces of nature. One that tends to keep immobile objects in place, **AND** another that keeps moving objects moving. This means that once you fight off the impulse to stay put, to do nothing, and start moving forward, you will be **the beneficiary** of inertia. It's like having the wind at your back.

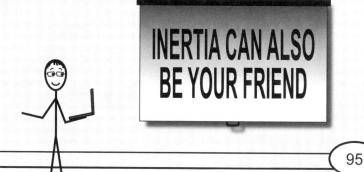

The point is that you can beat procrastination. After all, procrastination is all in your mind. While there are challenges you will face in life that are not within your control, fighting off procrastination is not one of those.

People who develop the mental strength and fortitude to deal with procrastination and the other challenges we all face are most likely to achieve their dreams.

PROCRASTINATION IS A DREAM KILLER.

97

Time management and mental fortitude go hand in hand.

Those who develop mental strength are more likely to:

(i) keep on schedule/plan;

(ii) make appropriate choices;

(iii) maintain good focus; and

(iv) defeat procrastination.

MENTAL FORTITUDE IS A SKILL THAT CAN BE DEVELOPED

98

I have studied mental fortitude for 25 years. I do not believe people are either born with it … or not. Rather I believe it is a skill that can be developed like any other.

Here are the three points to understand in order to begin developing strong mental fortitude:

1. **You are not your mind**. Rather, you are the higher being hearing your thoughts. As a result, you have a dominion over negative thoughts in your head – thoughts for example of procrastination or laziness.

Eckhart Tolle, makes this point in *The Power of Now*:

"The single most important step you can take is to learn to dis-identify from your mind. At some point you will smile at the thoughts in your mind, as if they are antics of a small child."

2. **Thoughts are things just like any other tangible item**. Napoleon Hill first made this point in 1936 (*Think & Grow Rich*). When you conceptualize a thought as a physical object, you control it. You can kick thoughts of procrastination right out of your mind, just like you would toss out of the house a misbehaving cat.

3. **Your brain can only process one dominant thought at a time**. When you feel a thought creeping into your mind, a negative impulse for example, train yourself to think of something else. A strong positive image or idea. Focusing on the positive thought will replace the negative thought, and your brain will thereby lose its negativity.

Let's now get into a little bitty of the nitty gritty of time management … I want to address specific ideas for using every hour you do have in the most powerful, effective way possible.

First and foremost I want to speak about clutter…. Yes, clutter. Clutter is the enemy of effectiveness.

100

This is how my garage used to look. It was totally cluttered. I could not find anything when I needed to. I had not yet learned the saying: *"A place for everything, and everything in its place."*

101

Then, one day, my wife had a suggestion. She told me that she would not speak to me until I cleaned the garage. So, I did.

102

And you know what? My wife did me a favor. Simply by getting rid of all the junk, the clutter, my garage became much more functional. I had room to exercise and meditate. I could actually find items that I had stored there. I could hold my classes.

The garage example is a metaphor. We all have both physical and mental clutter in our lives. It may be in your garage, or on your desk, or in your mind – that sense of being overwhelmed by too much to do. Wherever, the act of discarding and organizing can be liberating.

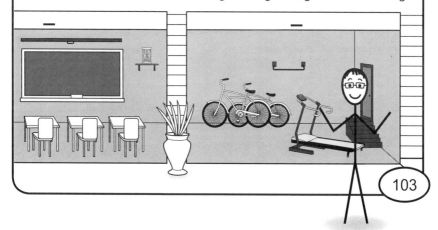

103

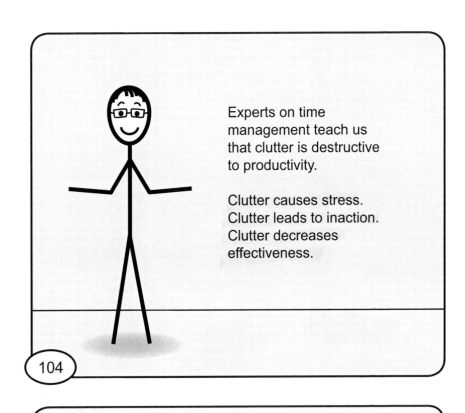

Experts on time management teach us that clutter is destructive to productivity.

Clutter causes stress. Clutter leads to inaction. Clutter decreases effectiveness.

104

Most of us have a brain like a vending machine. You put a couple of things in and then something falls out.

Time management experts suggest that by developing tangible systems to process and retain what we need to do, we give the brain a rest. It no longer has to struggle to deal with all the incoming stimuli, or to remember everything you need to accomplish.

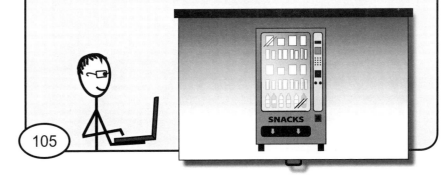

105

"The short-term memory part of your mind – the part that tends to hold all of the incomplete, undecided, and unorganized "stuff" – functions like a RAM on a personal computer. As with the RAM, there's limited capacity; there's only so much 'stuff' you can store in there and still have that part of your brain function at a high level. Most people walk around with their RAM bursting at the seams. They're constantly distracted, their focus disturbed by their own internal mental overload."

Getting Things Done, David Allen
(Penguin, 2001)

The quote above is from David Allen, one of our country's top thinkers on the subjects of time management and productivity.

Allen suggests that by developing good techniques and systems for collecting and storing information, we can develop a "mind like water."

A "mind like water?"

When Allen proposes that you want "a mind like water," he is suggesting a mind free of clutter. Think of a calm lake on a beautiful sunny day. No ripples. No waves. An easy serenity. By developing systems for processing and retaining information, you free your mind for important functions like analysis and creativity.

Here is my summary of the most important techniques for effective time management from David Allen's excellent book, *Getting Things Done – The Art of Stress-Free Productivity*:

1. Make your work area attractive and equip it with everything you need to work. You should enjoy spending time in your work area. Everything you want and need should be near at hand.

2. Create a filing system. Just the act of putting all material relevant to a particular subject in one place (file) is a huge step toward better time management and organization.

3. Develop ONE list where you write or type EVERYTHING that requires your attention. By trying to remember too much, you clutter your brain. The point is to get it out of your mind and down on paper.

4. Move every item. As much as possible, every piece of paper, every e-mail, text or voice message should be acted on when you first see or hear it. Don't leave anything "for later."

5. Exercise one of three choices for every item. Make a decision to: (i) act on it immediately, (ii) toss or delete it, or (iii) incorporate it into your one list for further action.

6. Convert thoughts to action steps. Don't write on your list "consider this" or "analyze that." Put down specific action steps. Instead of "consider this," put down exactly what you will do (for example): "(i) read about ___, (ii) speak with Bill about ___, (iii) make decision about ___."

7. Once you decide on action steps, take action if possible. As to anything that you can do in two minutes or less, do it now.

8. Maintain a good "tickler" system. Any reliable method that reminds you what you need to do and when, is fine.

9. Review weekly your systems for retention and productivity. Are your systems working as well as they should? Are you still burdened by trying to remember too much? Make changes as needed.

10. At least once a month, revisit your long-term goals. Are you making the right choices on a regular basis to move yourself closer to your goals? Or, are you spinning your wheels? Make sure you are moving in the right direction!

By clearing the mind, good things happen. Here I am on a sailing vacation I took last month. Away from the meetings, the cell phone, the blackberry and other daily stresses, I was quite productive. I wrote every morning, and I liked what I wrote.

This is me last night after dinner. As you can see, I am trying to do too much at once. This is another form of clutter – trying to jam too much activity into too little time or space.

Sometimes time and effectiveness are counterintuitive. There are many times when you accomplish more by trying to do less. Remember that thought as we will come back to it, but first I would like to bring up a new topic – PLANNING.

Planning simply means deciding **in advance** exactly what it is that you need to do in a given time period.

Many of us hate to plan. We live in such an action-packed society that we hurry around doing, doing, doing, and never step back to analyze what exactly is it that we are doing … AND WHY.

Perhaps you have heard the semi-humorous expression, READY, FIRE, AIM. That expression describes how many of us go about our days.

READY, FIRE, AIM

The problem with READY, FIRE, AIM of course is that energy is consumed "shooting" BEFORE the target is identified. That is **not** the right approach.

Instead, our objective should be to use our energy as effectively as possible by considering **in advance** where, when and how we wish to take action.

That means planning!

EVERY HOUR OF PLANNING IS WORTH FIVE IN EXECUTION

You should spend at least ten minutes to plan each of your days. If you are a night person, do it the night before. If you are a morning person, do it the morning of.

Ask yourself questions like:

What is it that I want to accomplish today?

How much time do I have to do that?

Can I defer doing some items which are not important to another day?

Is there a logical order to doing what I need to get done?

By taking just ten minutes to reflect on what it is that you want to accomplish, and how you are going to do so, you can dramatically improve the odds that **what you want to happen will, in fact, happen.**

As to planning your day, here's a new word you have probably not heard of... just give me a second to type this.

So what is **batching**? Many efficiency experts suggest that when you plan your day, you aggregate items that can be done at the **same time or place or manner**.

For example, let's say that you have to drive across town to accomplish X. You originally thought you'd do that around lunch time. But, when you started planning the day, you recalled that later in the day you need to be across town to pick up Y. And, when you consider doing X and Y, you reflect on Z – a meeting you will be having across town in 2 days. You decide that X and Y can wait, and 2 days from now you take one trip across town to accomplish X, Y and Z.

You have batched these three chores into one trip – saving you lots of time.

The point of batching, which is a subset of planning, is to think about ways to aggregate chores in a manner that allows you to accomplish them in less time than if you did each one on a separate schedule.

A close cousin of planning is preparation.

Edison said that "success is 90% perspiration and 10% inspiration." I would like to suggest that "success is 75% perspiration, 15% preparation and 10% inspiration."

On the screen is a mantra I use to remind myself of the importance of preparation.

By thinking ahead, by preparing, you are likely to reduce the effort you will need to complete whatever task is in front of you. To use a woodcutter metaphor – by sharpening your axe ahead of time – you reduce the energy you need to do your chopping.

PREPARATION
REDUCES
PERSPIRATION

Sometimes I even prepare for important meetings or phone calls. I know that during these meetings or calls I will have a limited amount of time to influence those in the room or on the phone. I want to use my time as powerfully as I can so decide **in advance** – the key points I want to make in the meeting or call.

In doing so, I try to create for myself the most effective meeting or conversation possible.

Just a few days ago, I even prepared for a "chance" encounter.

I knew that I was going to be in an office suite where a man I had been trying to meet had an office. I had a rough sense of his schedule. My goal was to try to find a way to "bump into" him and ask for five minutes of his time.

And so I prepared by orchestrating how we might "bump" into each other. I prepared by thinking through what I would say to him when we did and, of course, how I would use our five minutes together if he were willing to give me some of his time.

As I happens, I got "lucky". My plan for meeting him worked, and he was gracious in giving me five minutes of his time.

Given how well prepared I was, I feel that I effectively presented my proposal to him. Time will tell what he'll do, but no matter what – with preparation – I moved the ball forward.

Important Person

As with most things in life, planning **taken to the extreme** can become a negative.

As Einstein said: "nothing happens until something moves."

Some people overindulge in the planning process. They analyze and analyze and analyze because that can be easier than actually making a decision. Sometimes this process masks a fear to take action. At some point you need to take action, or at least make a decision that action is not the right course. Then move on.

ANALYSIS PARALYSIS

"Take time to deliberate, but when time for action arrives, stop thinking and go in."

Napoleon Bonaparte

AND NOW ON TO A REALLY BIG TOPIC:

TO DO LISTS

The physical product which manifests all your planning and preparation is the To Do List.

I am pleading with you: PLEASE START MAKING TO DO LISTS!

Do you remember David Allen's point about "a mind like water?" He maintained that the calmer your mind, the more productive you would be. And he proposed that one way to develop a calm mind was to create systems for collecting and processing information.

That is the point of a To Do List. It is simply a system by which you collect and manage – in one place – everything that you need to remember on a going forward basis.

There are many ways to create a To Do List. I happen to type my To Do List every morning as soon as I get up. Since much of my List from the prior day carries over, I am not crafting a new List every day. Rather I am revisiting the List from the day before and reworking it for the day ahead.

Many people use pen and paper to create a To Do List. Others use a cell phone notepad.

What counts is that you engage in a process of identifying what you need to do each day, and how and when you are going to do each task.

"Every effective executive works from a daily list. It is the most powerful tool ever discovered for maximum productivity.

When you create your daily list, you begin by writing down every single task you intend to complete over the course of the day. The rule is that you will increase your efficiency by 25 percent the very first day that you start using a list. This means that you will get two extra hours of productive time in an eight-hour day ... You can bring order out of chaos faster with a list than with any other time management tool."

Time Power: A Proven System for Getting More Done, Brian Tracy

1. Organization Effectiveness
2. Stress Reduction
3. Rechecking Goals and Priorities
4. Creativity

There are many reasons To Do Lists work:

First, by forcing yourself to make a To Do List, you are organizing your time. You are thinking through all that you need to get done and writing it down. By thinking about what needs to be done and what doesn't, you create a framework for your day.

Second, a very important reason for making a To Do List is that by doing so you reduce your stress. One cause of stress is the pressure you feel when you worry that there are things you're forgetting to do. When you organize your days, your stress may be reduced just by seeing your day visually – as opposed to grappling with all the pieces floating in your mind.

Third, making a To Do List requires you to rethink how you are spending your time and why. You will of course remember our discussion about goals and choices. Making a To Do List is a daily exercise in goal setting and choice making.

Fourth, making a To Do List can actually be fun. Think of it as writing a mini-novel with the main character being YOU. What you list is an act of creative planning – since the subject matter is YOU, your creative juices are heightened. You never know what thought or idea might arise out of the mere act of making a To Do List.

My wife thinks I can get a little obsessive about exercise. I just figured that while you were contemplating your To Do List, I would use the gap in time.

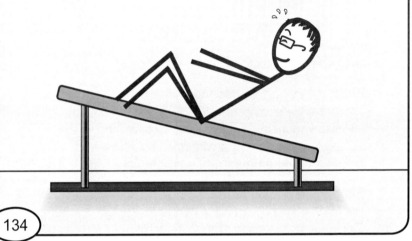

Whew ... OK, now I want to introduce a new concept to our panoply of "P" words. Part and parcel of preparation and planning is another P word.

Want to take a guess what it is?

My guess is ... prioritizing.

YES! You got it!

That's the next important concept we need to discuss.

We all have tons and tons of things to do. Prioritizing means selecting among all these items, and identifying what we should do first, then second ... and so on.

A lot of well-known thinkers have addressed the subject of prioritizing. One of my favorite is Stephen Covey who wrote *The 7 Habits of Highly Effective People*.

Before we speak to Covey's views on prioritizing, however, let's address what I consider the most important takeaway from his book.

Covey teaches us that success is not an accident. Rather, success is the result of repeatedly doing those things that optimize the probability of a favorable outcome.

Successful people increase their odds of a desired outcome by developing positive regimens and habits ... by creating behavioral patterns conducive to favorable results.

Let me give you a somewhat simple example.

I used to always lose my car keys in my house. That was due to the fact I would put them down wherever I was when I emptied my pockets. But sometimes, the next day, I forgot where that was.

Then one day I decided that no matter where I was in my house when I emptied my pockets, I would **always** put my car keys on the dresser in my bedroom. Just that little act, that regimen in my day, has saved me tons of time and energy since I no longer waste time looking for my car keys.

140

Perhaps my car key example seems a bit pedestrian. But the overall point is not. When we develop routines in our lives, we do two things:

1. We cut down on wasted motion (like spending time looking for car keys); and

2. We preserve energy by reducing deliberation. As an example, I try to exercise the same days and times every week. By fixing into my schedule (and mind) a definite time for exercise, I do not waste energy debating with myself as to whether (and when) to exercise. My exercise program becomes a regular part of my week, like brushing my teeth.

141

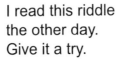

I read this riddle the other day. Give it a try.

"We are your constant companions, we are your greatest helpers or heaviest burdens.

We are completely at your command. Half of the things you do you might as well just turn over to us, and we will be able to do them quickly and correctly.

We are easily managed; but you must be firm with us.

Show us exactly how you want something done and after a few lessons we will do it automatically.

We are the servant of all great men and women – and of all failures as well.

We are not a machine, though we work with the precision of a machine.

You may run us for profit or for ruin – it makes no difference to us.

Train us, be firm with us and we will put the world at your feet. Be easy with us and we will destroy you.

WHAT ARE WE???"

HABITS

OK, now for Covey's views on prioritizing. Covey maintains that too many people prioritize by **reaction – doing what is pressing on them –** rather than by **proaction – doing what is important**.

Covey illustrates his point with a quadrant.

Covey recommends that when you are developing your To Do List, you put each task in one of these four quadrants:

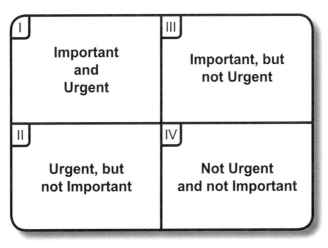

| I Important and Urgent | III Important, but not Urgent |
| II Urgent, but not Important | IV Not Urgent and not Important |

145

Then he suggests you prioritize.

And here is the question:

IN WHICH **SEQUENCE** WILL YOU PERFORM THE QUADRANTS?

146

The answer is:

First of course, you do the items in Quadrant I – the important, urgent items.

What's next is interesting … Covey says that the next quadrant in sequence should be Quadrant III – the one containing tasks that are important **but not urgent**.

The next box to address is Quadrant II – the one containing the chores that are urgent but not important.

And finally, of course, Quadrant IV – which is neither urgent nor important.

RECAP

1. In developing To Do Lists, we need to always balance urgent items against important items, and select the important over the urgent whenever possible.

2. Successful time management requires PROACTION instead of REACTION. We all tend to get up in the morning and start **reacting** – checking e-mails or voice messages, dealing with issues that may have come up over night. Instead we should be **proacting** – taking action steps that will move us forward, closer to our goals and objectives.

The difference in effectiveness between a proactive person and a reactive person is the difference between day ... and night.

There are several different methods for prioritizing the items on your To Do Lists.

I have personally been influenced by a book written in 1973 by Alan Lakein, *How to Take Control of Your Time and Life*. This excellent book suggests that at the beginning of every day you contemplate what you need to get done, and grade each item either an A, a B or a C. Then, as you start the day, you perform first the items graded A, then B, then C. Sometimes you never get to B and C.

Here is what my To Do List for today looks like:

Prepare for Time Management lecture	A
Call dentist to make appointment	B
Pick up more printer paper	B
Buy new running shoes	C
Thank you notes to reviewers of Skinny books	B
Rewrite 25 pages of Skinny on Entrepreneurship	A
Call John to discuss weekend plans	C

First and foremost I wanted to prepare for today's lecture to be sure your one hour with me was productive and entertaining. Then I wanted to write 25 more pages for my next book. I may not get to all the B and C items but that is OK with me so long as I give myself enough time to do all the A items to the best of my ability.

"I cannot emphasize strongly enough: you must set priorities. Some people do as many items as possible on their lists. They get a high percentage of tasks done, but their effectiveness is low because the tasks they've done are mostly C-priority. Others like to start at the top of the list and go right down it, again with little regard to what's important. The best way is to take your list and label each item according to the ABC priority ... then polish off the list accordingly."

How to Get Control of Your Time and Your Life
Alan Lakein (Signet, 1973)

Another writer I enjoy, Brian Tracy, has written a book titled *Eat That Frog*. His book suggests that in sequencing, in deciding what it is that you do when, you always tackle your hardest project first.

"Mark Twain once said that if the first thing you have to do each morning is to eat a live frog, you can go through the day with the satisfaction of knowing that is probably the worst thing that is going to happen to you all day long.

(My) rule of frog eating is this: If you have to eat two frogs, eat the ugliest one first.

This is another way of saying that if you have two important tasks before you, start with the biggest, hardest, and most important task first. Discipline yourself to begin immediately, and then to persist until the task is complete before you go on to something else."

All of the different approaches to prioritizing are, of course, easier to talk about than to implement. Sometimes urgent just overwhelms important. Sometimes C tasks must be addressed before A tasks. And some people don't function well if they have to tackle their hardest chore first – they need to clear the day of all the easier items before they have the fortitude to take on something really difficult.

Prioritizing forces you to make choices. There is an expression that "the squeaky wheel gets the grease." It means that sometimes the person or chore that makes the most immediate or noisiest demand gets attention. In prioritizing you cannot let those tasks or obligations making the "most noise" consume your attention. You must make deliberate decisions about what actions will take you closest to your objectives, and do those first.

There is a concept similar to prioritizing that I call streamlining.

Streamlining is about accomplishing more by doing less. An advocate of streamlining is a man named Leo Babauta. Babauta believes that the best way to accomplish a goal is to work **exclusively** at that goal until you complete it. And, only then, attack your next goal.

"There's never been an age in which we were so overwhelmed with information and tasks, so overloaded with e-mails and things to read and watch, so stressed by the incredible demands of our lives.

I'm a firm believer in simplicity. … Do less, not more, but achieve more because of the choices I make. Simplicity boils down to two steps: 1. Identify the essential. 2. Eliminate the rest.

I focus all of my energy and attention on that one challenge, and the barriers would break down. I'd focus on one goal at a time … and not try to accomplish everything at once."

**The Power of Less, Leo Babauta
(Hyperion 2009)**

Leo Babauta has a point. Sometimes when we try to do too much, we accomplish less than we otherwise might.

• • •

"The hurrier I go, the more I fall behind."

Anonymous

Remember the photo of me trying to clear the table? Ten seconds after that picture was taken I spent 20 minutes cleaning the kitchen floor.

The lesson, whether speaking about prioritizing or streamlining, is to be careful that you are not just being busy – in the place of, effective.

EFFECTIVE BEATS BUSY EVERY TIME.

See the guy up on the screen. His name is Tim Ferriss, and he wrote an excellent book, *The Four Hour Work Week*.

In his book, Ferriss emphasizes the point that too many people confuse having a lot to do with doing things that take you closer to your goals (effectiveness).

"In the strictest sense you shouldn't be trying to do more in each day, trying to fill every second with a work fidget of some type. It took me a long time to figure this out. I used to be very fond of the results-by-volume approach.

The intention ... is personal productivity."

The Four Hour Work Week

Ferriss makes an important distinction between busy-ness and effectiveness.

Ferris suggests that those who are scrambling all day – from one activity to the other – may, in fact, be keeping busy at the expense of being productive. The goal is productive – the doing of those things that are going to move you closer to your goals.

One last point on being busy. There are times in most of our lives when being busy is a refuge. By keeping ourselves busy, we "can't find" the quiet time needed to reflect on difficult choices. We may know, for example, we are in a situation that needs to change and yet, we create busy-ness so to avoid making a hard decision. I know I have done that at times.

Just something to think about.

BEING BUSY LEAVES NO TIME FOR SELF-REFLECTION

163

OK, now on to another hugely important rule about time management and personal effectiveness:

THE 80-20 RULE.

164

THE 80-20 RULE IS RIGHT UP THERE IN IMPORTANCE WITH THE GOLDEN RULE

To productivity and time management experts, it is perhaps as important as the Golden Rule.

The 80-20 rule goes like this:

20% of your actions will produce 80% of your results.

Let me elaborate.

People in many different fields understand that 80% of what they accomplish usually comes from about 20% of what they do. For example, salespeople know that 80% of their revenue often comes from 20% of their accounts. Investors know that 80% of their gains come from 20% of their investments. And so on.

The key – and here is where the rule gets challenging – is knowing exactly which of your actions and efforts are the critical 20% from which you will get you the big results.

The 80-20 rule was first identified in 1906 by an economist named Pareto. One day, while tending to his garden, Pareto realized that 80% of his most-edible vegetables were coming from only 20% of his plants. So he put more of his attention to caring for the high-producing plants, and the output from his garden increased greatly. No extra work: he just reduced the energy he was giving those plants that were not so productive, and reallocated it to the better plants.

That is why the 80-20 rule is so important. It does not require more work. Just smarter work.

People ask me how to incorporate the 80-20 rule into their lives. Here is how I respond:

Tell me one of your goals.

Tell me 5 things you are doing to achieve that goal.

Which of those 5 things is most likely to help you achieve that goal?

That's the thing to give your most energy and attention to.

In other words, if you are getting a lot of result ("80%") out of one or two activities ("20%"), those are what you should focus on. Please note that the actual percentage numbers are not relevant. What matters is the concept: some activities pay back more than others; put most of your energies toward those that give you the "biggest bang for the buck."

OK, how about we take a break?

Time for a little joke.

A father goes to visit his son in college. He is dismayed to see that his son has no clock or other visible time keeper in his dorm room.

Father: "Son, why is there no clock in your dorm room?"

Son: "Sure there is, dad, it's right there on the wall."

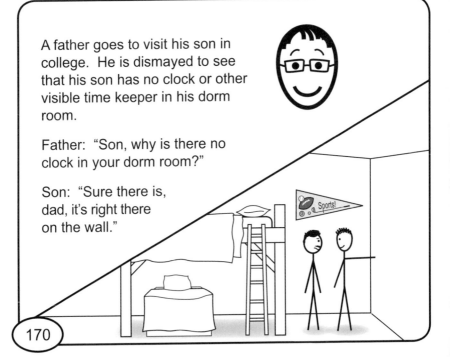

Sports!

Funny, heh?

Stick people are not that physically impressive so we have to be really clever.

Alrighty then, now for another really important topic – FOCUS.

If you want to get the most out of every free hour that you have, you need to learn to focus … to intensify the power of your mind by training it to concentrate on just one subject at a time.

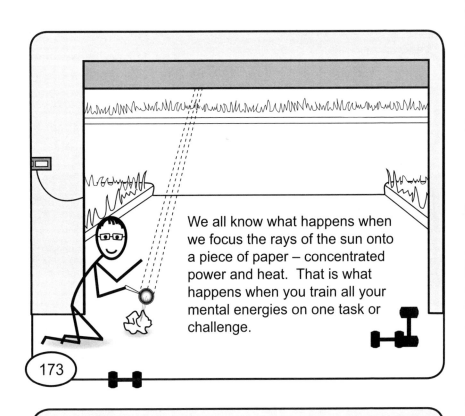

We all know what happens when we focus the rays of the sun onto a piece of paper – concentrated power and heat. That is what happens when you train all your mental energies on one task or challenge.

173

I have observed lots of successful people over the years and when they focus, they really focus. They put all their creative energies into accomplishing whatever it is they are working on … then they … UH OH … OH NO …

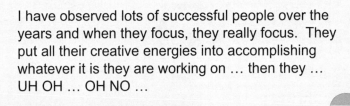

FOCUS...FOCUS FOCUS

174

OK, no harm… just a little smoke. Sorry about that but in truth my little accident is not a bad segue to talking about focus. Over time, as you develop your ability to focus, you will find that you stop hearing noises like sirens and dogs barking. Your mind is so trained on one subject that you may miss sounds and events going on around you. That's generally OK so long as your house is not on fire.

FOCUS…FOCUS
FOCUS

If you want to get the benefits of powerful focus, you need to limit distractions – interruptions that take your mind away from what you are doing. You need to keep all of your mental energies concentrating on the task or challenge at hand.

FOCUS…FOCUS
FOCUS

The number of potential distractions in your life is infinite. One possible distraction is people. People wanting to e-mail or text you, call you, sell you something, or meet with you. And right next to other people, the biggest potential impediment to focus is you – your own inability to keep your mind on just one thing when there are so many other cool things to do.

179

"*When walking, walk.
When eating, eat.*"

Zen Proverb

180

Want to improve your focus when you are working?

Remove distractions. **Cut down on interruptions**. Here are some suggestions:

DISTRACTIONS:

1. Log off the internet.
2. Shut off your cell phone.
3. Shut off all e-mail dings.
4. Pull the plug on the TV.
5. Remove any electronic product (e.g. video game) from the area.

INTERRUPTIONS:

1. If possible, close the door where you are working.
2. If that is not possible and other people are around:

   a) Wear a baseball cap with the visor pulled down so to appear unfriendly,

   b) Avoid eye contact with passers-by,

   c) Wear earphones (even if nothing is playing), and

   d) Put a box of Kleenex next to you, with several crumpled pieces nearby suggesting you have a cold.

AND SO ON.

DISTRACTIONS AND INTERRUPTIONS KILL FOCUS

A friend of mine, with an office near mine, drops in on me when he is bored.

I tried to give him hints when I was not in the mood for chatting but he missed the clues.

These days I am a bit more direct. When engaged and he drops in, I walk out of my office. He follows. Then I do a quick U-turn and close the door.

I do not of course want to offend my friend. But, at times, in order to protect your ability to focus, you need to say NO to personal interruptions. Anyone that takes your mind off what you are doing when you are trying to focus needs to learn to wait until you are free.

184

Don't think you can focus when you are multi-tasking.

Let me be very clear about multi-tasking: when you try to do more than one thing at a time, you dilute the effectiveness of each thing you are doing. Those who multi-task, and think they are doing each thing well, are only fooling themselves.

DON'T FOOL YOURSELF BY MULTI-TASKING

185

"While you can hold several chunks of information in mind at once, you can't perform more than one conscious process at a time with these chunks – without impacting performance. ... While it is physically possible sometimes to do several mental tasks at once, accuracy and performance drop off quickly.

(T)he scientist Harold Pashler showed that when people do two cognitive tasks at once, their cognitive capacity can drop from that of a Harvard MBA to that of an eight-year-old. It's a phenomenon called dual-task interference. ... The lesson is clear: if accuracy is important, don't divide your attention."

Your Brain at Work, David Rock
(Harper Collins, 2009)

Multi-taskers are supplanting focus with tumult. And that's a shame because when you really put all of your creative juices and personal energies onto one task – and one task only – the sky's the limit as to what you can accomplish.

Let me give you a few examples of what some people have accomplished – in incredibly short periods of time – when they put **all** of their energy to the challenge in front of them.

1. Pablo Picasso painted his most famous painting, Guernica, in less than two months. He was inspired to paint this great work after the bombing of his hometown (Guernica) in Spain during World War II.

2. Sylvester Stallone wrote the screenplay to Rocky in three days. Movie of the Year in 1980, *Rocky* spawned a whole series of *Rocky* movies and made Stallone an international star – changing his entire life in a flash.

"Now is the time to grab life by the throat and don't let go."

Sylvester Stallone

3. In 1987 the lead guitarist of the band, Guns N' Roses, Slash, spent three hours writing a song titled *Welcome to the Jungle*. This song became hugely popular and in 2009, VH1 named it the greatest hard rock song ever recorded.

4. In an amazing sports comeback, with 27 minutes left in the football game and trailing 35 to 3 in the 1993 NFL Playoffs, the Buffalo Bills rallied – scoring 38 points to win the game 41 to 38!!

Time is a gift. It is your opportunity to make something great happen. To illustrate your unique talents. To change your life.

Every day we get twenty-four 60-minute gifts to do something terrific.

Even one hour – let alone a day, a week or more – is a very powerful palette when it is the recipient of all of your attention.

189

"If you ever want to get something done, ask the busiest person you know."

Anonymous

190

Wow! I can't believe it... we are coming to the end of our hour. I hope the time flew by for you as quickly as it flew by for me.

Just before we break, I want to list my favorite techniques and strategies for improving your effectiveness and time management.

191

JIM'S FAVORITE TECHNIQUES FOR IMPROVING EFFECTIVENESS AND TIME POTENCY

A. Discard
B. Make immediate decisions
C. Create filing systems
D. Select specific times to respond to calls/e-mails
E. Use a watch with a second-hand display
F. Carry a note-taker
G. Learn to scan
H. Ask for help
I. Finish in one sitting
J. Move on – what's done is done

192

A. Learn to discard quickly and without guilt. Pack rats hate this one. Learn to throw things away. To delete e-mails. More stuff means more junk and more clutter. The quicker you discard, the quicker you move on.

B. As to every item that comes into your day, make an immediate decision what to do with it. Whether a text, an e-mail, a voice message, a letter … whatever. Either: a) act on the item, b) discard it, or c) save it. Resist the impulse to "deal with it later." A subset of this technique is the suggestion to "touch every paper just once."

C. Put every piece of paper, book or article that pertains to a single project in one place. For me, when I am starting to write a Skinny book I find that the act of putting all my research into one box calms me down and helps me organize my thoughts.

The book you are reading today looked like this 60 days before publication.

D. Pick one or two times a day to answer voice messages, texts or e-mails. If you are working and allow yourself to be interrupted by continual pulls on your time, you will never get anything done well. Experts believe that when people are productively engaged, and then interrupted, it takes them 5 – 10 minutes to get back into productive thought after the interruption.

E. I recommend you wear a runner's watch with a digital second-hand display. There is no better way I know of to keep you focused on the passage of time!

F. Keep handy some mechanism for taking down ideas that pop into your head during the day. By doing so you help reduce the stress caused by worrying that you will forget something you need to do.

G. Teach yourself to speed read. Like mental fortitude, speed reading is a skill that can be developed. Here is the single most important point to understand about speed reading:

YOU DO NOT NEED TO READ EVERY WORD OF WHATEVER IT IS YOU ARE READING (EXCEPT SKINNY BOOKS OF COURSE).

You can usually get the intent of the writing by reading about 50% of the words.

For me, some combination of the following techniques gives me what I need to know:

(i) read just the first sentences of every paragraph,

(ii) read all words that are in bold, underlined or italicized,

(iii) read just the introductory and conclusory chapters or paragraphs,

(iv) scan vertically; not horizontally,

(v) read without mouthing any words (as best as you can), and

(vi) don't reread until you finish a page or several paragraphs, and only if you are convinced you missed something.

"The average reader can increase, by a minimum of three times, his present reading rate. (Speed) reading is a skill – a developed or acquired ability."

Triple Your Reading Speed, **Wade Cutler (Pocket Books, 4th Edition, 2002)**

H. Never hesitate to ask for help. You can cut a lot of time out of any project by finding someone who has done it before, and asking their guidance. No sense in reinventing the wheel.

Whatever you are doing, someone has most likely done before. If you can find such a person and convince them to guide you, you are certainly going to save yourself a lot of time and heartache.

I. Whenever possible, finish a task in one sitting or segment of time.

Parkinson's Law says that a project will expand to the limits of the time in which one has to do it. If you have three hours to finish a project, you will finish in three hours. If you have a week, it will take you a week and most likely the finished product will not be appreciably better.

J. Move on. After you complete a test, a book, a project or even a day, stop thinking about it. It's over. That's yesterday's news. Do not waste precious energy hashing over what might have been.

"I don't ever remember missing a single foul shot."

Of course Shaq has missed a lot of foul shots. But, the second after he missed one, he forgot about it. This is a very important talent to develop. The past is over. Right now is a gift. That's why they call it the present.

> *"Nothing ever happened in the past; ... Past and future obviously have no reality of their own. ... their reality is 'borrowed' from Now."*

The Power of Now, Eckhart Tolle
(Namaste, 1999)

Well this concludes our session.

I hope you won't think of time management as a chore. Think of it as fun … like any challenge, something to be worked at but which can lead to great results once mastered!

The following pages summarize the ten most important concepts to remember about effective time management.

Thanks for stopping by. I enjoyed having you as my guest!!

THE
TEN MOST
IMPORTANT
POINTS
TO REMEMBER
ABOUT TIME
MANAGEMENT

1. SELF-AWARENESS IS THE *SINE QUA NON*.

You can't go anywhere with time management until you are aware of how you are spending your time.

I recommend keeping a time journal for a week or so. Watch for areas where you might re-allocate your time expenditures.

2. GOAL-SETTING IS THE FIRST STEP.

There is no point to worrying about the passage of time unless and until you have identified those goals or objectives you are trying to achieve.

You are flying blind until you know the direction in which you should be traveling.

3. CHOICES ARE TOUGH.

Time management is ultimately about making choices.

You are gifted 24 hours every day. 168 hours every week. How you choose to use those hours is up to you.

Goal achievement is about making hard choices. About deciding among many competing demands on your time.

4. YOU CAN "CREATE" TIME.

Watch for ways to turn unproductive time into productive time. Look for gaps in your day or week when you can use time productively instead of sitting on your rump waiting for something to happen.

Increase your energy with exercise and healthy eating. The more energy you bring to an hour, the more powerful that hour becomes in moving you toward the realization of your goals.

5. PROCRASTINATION IS THE ENEMY.

Procrastination is so darn tempting. But, you must fight the impulse.

Try to think of yourself as either in forward or reverse. Either you are moving toward your goal which is good, or away from you goal. When you are standing still, your goal is most likely moving away from you.

6. AIM FOR "A MIND LIKE WATER."

If you can declutter your work area, your life and eventually your mind, you increase your effectiveness dramatically.

Clutter is an impediment to productive, powerful thought.

When you declutter your mind, you liberate it!

7. PLANNING AND PREPARATION ARE WORTH THE EFFORT.

By contemplating in advance what you want to accomplish with a particular event or in a specific time period, you increase the prospect that you will achieve what you set out for.

210

8. WHEN YOU PRIORITIZE, YOU SEPARATE THE WHEAT FROM THE CHAFF.

Prioritizing means deciding what you are going to do when.

By organizing your day and life in terms of what matters most, you increase the probability that you will get to where you want to go.

One way to prioritize is to remember the 80/20 rule, which says that 20% of your activities will result in 80% of the progress toward your goals.

211

9. SINGLE-MINDED FOCUS IS WHERE IT'S AT.

By cutting down distractions and bringing lasered focus to the task at hand, you multiply the power of your effort exponentially.

Distractions are dream killers. They dilute your braininess. When you decide to work, then work, and do not let interruptions from third parties interfere with the effort.

212

10. PICK AND CHOOSE THE TIME MANAGEMENT TECHNIQUES THAT WORK FOR YOU.

We have identified time management techniques that increase efficiency. Some may make sense to you, others not.

Experiment and try different ideas. The key is to strive to use every hour you have as effectively as possible.

213

The End!

CONCLUSION

We here at **The Skinny On**™ hope you enjoyed this book. We would love to hear your comments.

My personal e-mail is jrandel@theskinnyon.com.

Thanks for your attention, and may time always be on your side!

Warm regards,

Jim Randel

FURTHER READING

Here's a list of some of the books we reviewed in preparing The Skinny on Time Management:

Break-Through Rapid Reading,
Peter Kump (Prentice Hall, 1998)

Creative Time Management,
Jan Yager (Hannacroix, 1999)

Eat That Frog!,
Brian Tracy Berrett-Koehler, 2007)

Future Shock,
Alvin Toffler (Bantam, 1970)

Getting Things Done,
David Allen (Viking, 2001)

How to Get Control of Your Time and Your Life, Alan Lakein (Signet, 1973)

Remember Everything You Read,
Stanley Frank (Avon, 1990)

Speed Reading for Professionals,
Wechsler and Bell (Barrons, 2006)

The 4-Hour Workweek,
Timothy Ferriss (Crown, 2007)

The 7 Habits of Highly Effective People, Stephen Covey (Simon & Schuster, 1989)

The 25 Best Time Management Tools & Techniques, Dodd and Sundheim (Peak Performance, 2005)

The Autobiography of Benjamin Franklin, Benjamin Franklin (1790)

The One Minute Manager, Blanchard and Johnson (William Morrow, 1982)

The Power of Focus, Canfield, Hansen, Hewitt (Health Communications, 2000)

The Power of Less, Leo Babauta (Hyperion, 2009)

The Time Trap, Mackenzie and Nickerson (AMACOM, 2009)

Time Power, Brian Tracy (AMACOM, 2007)

Triple Your Reading Speed,
Wade Cutler (Pocket Books, 2002)

Work Less, Do More,
Jan Yager (Sterling, 2008)

Pssst ... get
the skinny on
life's most
important lessons

Remember to
visit theskinnyon.com and join
The Skinny On™ community to:

- Keep your book current
  with free web updates

- Sign up for **The Skinny On™**
  e-letter

- View upcoming topics and
  suggest areas of research
  for new titles

- Read excerpts from any of
  The Skinny On™ books

- Purchase other **The Skinny On™**
  titles

- Learn how to write for
  The Skinny On™!

Connect with us on:

www.theskinnyon.com